Little Leaders

VISIONARY WOMEN

AROUND

THE WORLD

VASHTI HARRISON

PUFFIN

PUFFIN BOOKS

UK | USA | Canada | Ireland | Australia
India | New Zealand | South Africa

Puffin Books is part of the Penguin Random House group of companies
whose addresses can be found at global.penguinrandomhouse.com.

www.penguin.co.uk www.puffin.co.uk www.ladybird.co.uk

Penguin
Random House
UK

First published in hardback in the USA by Little, Brown and Company and in Great Britain by Puffin Books 2018
001
Copyright © Vashti Harrison, 2018
The moral right of the author/illustrator has been asserted
Printed in China
A CIP catalogue record for this book is available from the British Library
ISBN: 978–0–241–34688–4
All correspondence to:
Puffin Books, Penguin Random House Children's, 80 Strand, London, WC2R 0RL

QUOTE SOURCES

26 'that a black woman can invent something for the benefit of humankind': Bessie Blount Griffin in the
Virginian-Pilot, September 9, 2008.

31 'A people's art is the genesis of their freedom': Claudia Jones in her pamphlet from the 1959 Carnival.

62 'for her contribution to sustainable development, democracy and peace': 'The Nobel Peace Prize 2004'.
Nobelprize.org.

TO ANYONE WHOSE

IDEAS HAVE BEEN CALLED

IMPRACTICAL, IDEALISTIC, GRANDIOSE,

WHIMSICAL, IMAGINATIVE OR CRAZY.

TO ANYONE WHO DARES

TO DREAM BIG.

Contents

Introduction

When we call someone a visionary, it's usually to suggest that they are some type of genius. We celebrate these people as the best of the best. We look to them as leaders, as beacons of inspiration and something to aspire to. But getting to that level of success takes a lot of hard work. It can take years of being misunderstood. Sometimes others just can't see the vision that these people are working towards. Some of them are called crazy; others, dreamers. Zaha Hadid spent years without her buildings being approved for construction because people didn't understand her designs. Esther Afua Ocloo was mocked for selling her homemade goods on the street. Eiko Ishioka was told the design world was not a place for girls. But each of them had a vision for her future – and she didn't let anything get in the way.

The women in this book looked at things differently. They saw things that no one else did. They asked questions no one else was asking. And they chose to do something about it. Often it took a long time for others to understand them or value their efforts. Many were simply ahead of their time, laying the groundwork for others. Some of them are still ahead of their time, but hopefully they will one day be recognized for their vision.

Through their curiosity and creative thinking, these ordinary women accomplished extraordinary things. Thanks to their persistence and willingness to make mistakes, they had a lasting impact on their fields of study, and some of them even changed the world.

I knew I wanted to fill this book with the stories of creative people, but I also wanted to challenge the idea of what creativity can be. It's a term commonly associated with artists rather than scientists. But both professions require critical thinking and inventiveness. I wanted to see the stories of all these people in the same place because when their efforts cross over, amazing things can happen. Sometimes art can be incredibly technical, as in the work of Monir Shahroudy Farmanfarmaian, and sometimes science can require a lot of imagination, as with Bessie Blount Griffin, a nurse turned inventor!

When I was young, I thought of the arts and sciences as completely different worlds. I knew I liked to draw and that I was good at maths, but never once did I believe the two could be used together. It didn't occur to me that drawing skills can be used in engineering, architecture and beyond! It wasn't until many years later that I realized I never needed to put myself into one box. What would have happened if I could have brought the two together sooner? Ada Lovelace would probably say it could lead to something incredible.

Ada believed in something she called poetical science. She suggested that if you separated art and science, you could never fully understand the essence of an idea. She didn't let her passions for art and science divide her – instead she came to understand that there was value in using both at the same time. When you look at the world with many points of view, it can lead to real innovation and create true potential for the future.

I hope these biographies inspire you to create, invent, imagine; to try new things; to make mistakes; to ask questions. In these pages, you'll learn about painters and print-makers, dancers and writers, microbiologists and chemists. The Little Leaders are here to guide you on this journey around the world, through space and time. Let them inspire your future!

Fatima Al-Fihri
Ninth Century

EDUCATIONAL PHILANTHROPIST
TUNISIA, MOROCCO

Not much is known about Fatima's life. She lived more than a thousand years ago! It was rare back then for a woman's story to be recorded, but Fatima left behind something pretty remarkable, so she will not be forgotten.

One of two daughters of a wealthy merchant, Fatima was both educated and devout. When she was a child, her family migrated from al-Qayrawan (in modern-day Tunisia) to Fes (in what is now Morocco). They were part of a large influx of people who brought a lot of business and culture to the city. But the majority of the new population was of Muslim faith – and there weren't enough mosques for everyone. Mosques are religious houses of worship that also serve as places for the community to gather. When Fatima's father passed away, he left her and her sister a large inheritance. Both sisters wanted to use the money to help their community. Fatima decided to use her part to build the biggest mosque in North Africa. She envisioned it not only as a faith centre, but also a madrassa – a place for study.

Fatima was interested in architecture and oversaw the whole construction of the building. Named for the city of her birth, Al Quaraouiyine opened in 859. Over the next few decades the curriculum grew to include the natural sciences as well as religion, making it the first degree-granting institution in the world and a model for future universities! Its impact carried far beyond Morocco, as it attracted scholars from all over, such as the scientific scholar Gerbert of Aurillac. He later became Pope Sylvester II – known for introducing Arabic numerals to medieval Europe!

In 1963 Al Quaraouiyine became an official state university in Morocco. In fact, it is the oldest operating university in the world. Long after she passed away, Fatima's vision lives on as scholars and the faithful continue to be educated there today.

Wang Zhenyi
1768–1797

ASTRONOMER, POET, MATHEMATICIAN
CHINA

Born into a family of scholars during the Qing dynasty, Zhenyi was fortunate to receive an education, rare for a girl in her time. Her grandfather had an extensive collection of books, something that was even rarer, since the emperor was strict about what was acceptable literature. She learned everything, from astronomy and maths to poetry. She didn't spend all her time indoors, though – she learned archery and equestrian arts as well.

Most of what we know about Zhenyi comes from her writings. She left behind twelve volumes of poems and many academic papers. She used her poetry to describe and critique the world around her. She often wrote about inequality between men and women, as well as other social injustices. If the emperor was strict about the books people could have, imagine how brave Zhenyi had to be to openly criticize him in her poetry!

Zhenyi especially loved the stars and published several volumes of maths and astronomy for beginners. In her day, many of the phenomena in the sky were commonly considered supernatural. She was confident there was a logical explanation for cosmic events, and she proved it by explaining eclipses. Using a table as Earth, a lamp as the sun and a mirror as the moon, she demonstrated that when the three bodies line up, either the moon blocks our view of the sun or Earth blocks the sun's light from reaching the moon, thus forming an eclipse.

Above all, she wanted to share her knowledge with people, so before she passed away she made sure all her poems and academic papers would be kept safe. Many were published after her death. Zhenyi made a life for herself that was not constricted by rules of what a woman could or could not be. She saw a world with limitless possibilities for girls and potential for anyone to have the freedom to study whatever they want.

Ada Lovelace
1815 – 1852

COMPUTER PROGRAMMER
ENGLAND

What happens when imagination and technology collide? Well, Ada herself was a physical embodiment of such a collision. Her father was the poet Lord Byron and her mother, Anne Isabelle Milbanke, loved maths. Perhaps the combination of her parents' sensibilities was what made Ada so special. Her unique view of the world meant that she didn't just dream of being a fairy – she also knew she'd need to devise a way to fly.

Ada grew up during the Industrial Revolution, a time when scientists and artists gathered to discuss new inventions and creations. At one such meeting, Ada saw the mathematician Charles Babbage demonstrate a mechanical adding machine. Ada asked Charles to mentor her, but he turned her down at first. He was working on something new: the Analytical Engine, inspired by mechanical looms used in the textile industry.

To prove herself to him, Ada translated an Italian article about his new machine into English. She added her own notes, making her translation nearly three times as long as the original article! She understood that the Analytical Engine could be programmed to do limitless tasks and described a formula for programming it to calculate a mathematical sequence of numbers known as the Bernoulli numbers. Ada had a vision of a general-purpose computer a century before anyone would build one.

Although Ada and Charles finally worked together, they never built the Analytical Engine. Ada's contributions went unappreciated until the 1950s, when her translation of the article was discovered. Her work on the Bernoulli numbers is considered the first-ever computer program, and made Ada the first computer programmer. Ada believed firmly in what she called 'poetical science', the synthesis of creativity and technology – and that human imagination could be combined with technology to kick-start the future.

Marie Curie
1867 – 1934

PHYSICIST, CHEMIST
POLAND, FRANCE

Marie grew up in Warsaw, Poland, when most of the country was ruled by an oppressive Russian government. She graduated at fifteen, but there was no place for her at the all-male universities. Desperate to further her education, she attended a 'flying university', a secret institution where women and patriotic Poles could learn. Finally, at twenty-four, after saving money and helping her sister get a degree, she studied at the University of Paris.

She worked hard to catch up with her classmates and eventually earned degrees in both physics and mathematics. She wanted to return to Poland to teach but was again turned away because she was a woman. She met a young scientist, Pierre, who was impressed with her – and in love with her. He begged her to stay in Paris, apply for a doctorate and marry him. She did.

In 1896 the physicist Henri Becquerel had discovered that uranium salts emitted an odd glow – and Marie wanted to know why. She found that the glowing persisted under every condition and concluded that the source must be atomic: the atoms of uranium have an unstable nucleus, so they emit particles and release energy. She called this radioactivity.

Pierre joined her research and together they discovered two new elements, which they named polonium (after her beloved homeland, Poland) and radium. In 1903 Marie, Pierre and Henri Becquerel were awarded the Nobel Prize in Physics. In 1911 Marie was awarded a second Nobel Prize, in Chemistry, for her further work on radioactive elements, which had a lasting impact on scientific research and discoveries in medicine. She was the first person to be awarded Nobel Prizes in two different fields.

Marie's list of accomplishments goes on and on – first female professor at the Sorbonne, helped prove that atoms are divisible, developed a portable X-ray device used during the First World War – but along the way she struggled to pay the bills. Still, Marie's passion kept her going, and her curiosity and unique vision led her to some of science's greatest discoveries.

Edith Head
1897 – 1981

COSTUME DESIGNER
UNITED STATES OF AMERICA

Edith had a lonely childhood. Her family moved around the American Southwest a lot, so she never had many friends. She often played by herself out on the dusty plains, but in her imagination the world came alive. Having neither toys nor dolls, she made figurines with wood from desert plants. She dressed them up with scraps of fabric and had tea parties with them, dreaming of a glamorous life. When the family moved to Los Angeles while Edith was in high school, it was a dream come true. She acted in plays, took art classes and developed a keen eye for design.

In 1923 Edith saw an advertisement for a job opening for a costume sketch artist at Paramount, one of the biggest studios in Hollywood. She applied, even though she didn't have the experience, and talked her way into the job. She quickly proved her talent, and by 1938 she was Paramount's chief costume designer. In her career Edith worked on over one thousand movies and was nominated for thirty-five Academy Awards. She won a record eight times.

Edith took special care to consult with the movie stars she was dressing. Her personal connection with them made her a standout asset to a film. Once she knew the performer's personality, she could create a costume that would help transform the actor into a character. Some of her most iconic looks were for Grace Kelly, Audrey Hepburn and Hedy Lamarr.

Edith herself had an iconic look, always sporting a chic hairdo with a bold fringe, round glasses and a wardrobe strictly in the colours black, white and beige.

Today, Edith is celebrated as one of Hollywood's greatest designers. Her talents took her outside of the film world as well: she penned two books on fashion and costume in Hollywood and designed uniforms for women in the US Coast Guard, leaving her mark on history beyond the silver screen.

Peggy Guggenheim
1898–1979

ART COLLECTOR, PHILANTHROPIST
USA, ITALY

Born into the wealthy Guggenheim family, heiress and socialite Peggy didn't dive into the art world until she was thirty-nine years old. Art collecting was not unfamiliar to her – her uncle Solomon was doing the same (he eventually founded the Guggenheim Museum in New York). She met the artist Marcel Duchamp, who mentored her in the art world. Although not an artist herself, carefree Peggy flourished in her new lifestyle, moving to Paris and making friends with artists, musicians and filmmakers.

In 1938 she opened her first gallery, the Guggenheim Jeune, in London, which exhibited contemporary and abstract art. She began to amass pieces for her own collection and soon set her sights on something bigger: opening a museum. Unfortunately, the Second World War was on the horizon. The Nazi regime in Germany disliked anything representing modern sensibilities and began destroying all the art they considered corrupt. Sensing the urgency of the situation, Peggy purchased as many paintings as she could – a painting a day – and smuggled them out of France.

Upon her return to the United States, Peggy opened the Art of This Century Gallery in New York City, where she exhibited all the paintings she had rescued: cubist, surrealist, and abstract works by artists now celebrated as masters. Their art might have been destroyed, but, thanks to Peggy, they are cemented in history.

Peggy championed artists and other creative individuals who were often overlooked. She gave Jackson Pollock his first show, and put up New York's first exhibition of contemporary female artists. Afterwards, she moved to Venice, Italy, and retired there with her personal collection. In 1951 she opened up her palazzo to allow visitors in, and today it is one of the most important museums of modern art in Italy.

Grace Hopper
1906-1992

NAVY ADMIRAL, COMPUTER SCIENTIST
UNITED STATES OF AMERICA

Grace always wanted to know how things worked. When she was seven, she dismantled her alarm clock just to figure out what was going on inside. Once she did, she easily put the clock back together! At college Grace studied maths and physics and later became a maths professor. She had a knack for explaining complicated concepts.

When the United States entered the Second World War, Grace wanted to help. The US Navy rejected her several times – once for being too small and once for being too old. But Grace persisted, and in 1943 she joined the US Naval Reserve through the WAVES (Women Accepted for Volunteer Emergency Service) programme. She was assigned to a special project: the navy hoped the Harvard Mark I, the first electromechanical computer in the United States, would provide calculations that could help win the war. But they needed someone to program it first. The computer (which was fifteen-and-a-half metres long!) was new to everyone but, as with her alarm clock, Grace figured it out. Her job was to write a book on how to use it – the first computer manual!

In 1949 Grace worked at a company overseeing the programming of the first commercial computer. Grace thought it would be easier if users could just communicate with it in English, but her co-workers laughed at the idea. Eventually she tried it, and her team ended up creating the precursor to COBOL, the most useful programming language ever.

When Grace was sixty, she returned to the navy to standardize computer languages. And when she retired at the age of seventy-nine, ending a landmark career, she was the oldest active-duty commissioned officer in the navy!

Perhaps Grace's greatest achievement was her translation of complicated ideas into simple language, something that opened up computing and coding for generations to come.

Frida Kahlo
1907–1954

PAINTER

MEXICO

Tragedy struck Frida throughout her life, but she channelled her pain into art. As a child, Frida contracted polio and one of her legs became withered. She walked with a limp for the rest of her life, but she disguised her disfigurement with beautiful long skirts associated with traditional Tehuana clothing. At eighteen, she was in a bus accident and endured a long recovery process. One thing she could do while bedridden? Paint. Her mother built an easel that hung above her hospital bed and, with nothing else to look at, Frida painted herself.

Her self-portraits were a mix of the exuberant, sad, colourful and dark. She painted not only what she saw but also what she felt, often using symbols to represent those feelings: nails could mean pain; a captured deer, vulnerability. Because of this, Frida is often associated with artists of the surrealism movement such as Salvador Dalí, who painted dreamlike worlds. But Frida never considered herself a surrealist, because she didn't paint dreams; she simply reflected all the realities she experienced and felt.

As she healed, Frida joined Mexico's artistic and political circles and met the famous muralist Diego Rivera. In 1929 they married, and together they travelled the world.

Many of Frida's paintings were self-portraits – her trademark impassive gaze drew viewers in and begged them to face tragedy and sadness as well as beauty. But her work wasn't always about herself. She had a revolutionary spirit and often incorporated her social and political opinions into her pieces. To communicate her strong passion for indigenous Mexicans, she embedded Aztec symbols into her paintings. Her distinctive wardrobe, too, reflected her identity. She chose the Tehuana style of dress not only for the long skirts but also because it represents female power. Frida showed Mexico as vibrant and beautiful, and she both celebrated its heritage and captured the fears and struggles of its people.

Gyo Fujikawa
1908–1998

ILLUSTRATOR
UNITED STATES OF AMERICA

As a child, Gyo could be found sketching flowers in her backyard in Berkeley, California, instead of playing with dolls or toys. Her creativity was evident early on, but her parents worried about their daughter's future if she chose a career in art. For Japanese immigrants in the early twentieth century, it was difficult to succeed. But Gyo persevered and earned a scholarship to the Chouinard Art Institute in Los Angeles.

After graduation, Gyo spent a year in Japan, studying the traditional art of brush painting. Back in California, she returned to Chouinard as a teacher. She also worked part-time for Walt Disney Productions, designing brochures and posters for its films – an impressive accomplishment in a company with few women or people of colour. This job took her to New York City in 1941.

That same year, after the Japanese attack on Pearl Harbor, the US entered the Second World War. Soon, Japanese Americans on the West Coast were forced into relocation camps. Gyo was fortunate to be in New York, so she avoided internment. Her family was not so lucky.

Despite the war, Gyo worked diligently. Eventually she left Disney and began illustrating magazine covers. This got her noticed by a book publisher, and she was hired to illustrate a new edition of Robert Louis Stevenson's *A Child's Garden of Verses*. In 1963 she published a book called *Babies*, which she wrote and illustrated herself, and soon followed that with *Baby Animals*. Both books were wildly successful and are still in print today. She eventually published more than forty books for children.

Athough she never had kids of her own, Gyo took special care in her work to consider what a child might enjoy. Her style is vibrant and elegant with sweet, round-cheeked characters. But what made Gyo's work historic was her choice to celebrate diversity and incorporate characters of many ethnicities into children's books.

CHOREOGRAPHER, ANTHROPOLOGIST
UNITED STATES OF AMERICA

Despite a strict upbringing, Katherine was a creative and enterprising child. At the age of twelve she published a short story in W. E. B. Du Bois's monthly magazine, and at fourteen she produced, directed and starred in a performance to raise money for her church. Dancing, though, was her true love, and she studied modern dance and ballet in her childhood. Everything changed for her after she attended a lecture on black culture at the University of Chicago. She learned that much of black culture in America – the music, folklore and dances – had all begun somewhere in Africa.

Katherine wanted to find out how the roots of African culture had spread around the world, so she began studying anthropology, focusing on dances from the African diaspora. Throughout her career she found a way to balance studying dance, teaching it and actually performing it. In the early 1930s she formed the Ballet Nègre, one of the first black ballet companies in the United States, and the Negro Dance Group, a school to teach young black dancers about their heritage.

In 1935 she received a grant from the Rosenwald Fund and a prestigious Guggenheim Fellowship to conduct an ethnographic study of dance in the Caribbean. She travelled to Jamaica, Martinique and Trinidad but truly connected with the culture in Haiti.

After Katherine returned to the United States, she founded the Dunham School of Dance and Theater. The dancers toured and performed and taught movement to artists, dancers and actors. Her classes were extremely popular due to her unique methods. She combined traditional African and Caribbean movements with ballet and modern dance in an innovative way that was soon canonized as the Dunham Technique. It's still taught in dance classes today, and she is referred to as the Matriarch of Black Dance.

Mary Blair
1911–1978

MODERN PAINTER AND COLOURIST
UNITED STATES OF AMERICA

Mary began her career as a watercolourist. She studied naturalist painting at the Chouinard Art Institute in Los Angeles, where she met Lee Blair. They fell in love and married, and soon their art styles were indistinguishable. The Great Depression was tough on their art careers, so Mary reluctantly followed Lee into the animation industry. Eventually they both landed jobs at Walt Disney's animation studio.

In 1941 President Roosevelt commissioned Walt Disney to participate in a trip to promote goodwill in South America on behalf of the United States. Walt gathered a group of artists to travel with him. Lee was selected. Mary was not. So she went to Walt's office and successfully made her bid. On the trip, Mary's style exploded! Her watercolours couldn't capture the vibrancy she saw, so she switched to gouache, a bright, chalky paint, and began working in a bolder, more whimsical style. She simplified her forms in a sweet, almost childlike way. By the end of the trip, Walt considered Mary his favourite artist.

After the Second World War, Disney hired Mary to do visual development on *Cinderella* (1950), *Alice in Wonderland* (1951) and *Peter Pan* (1953). Her colour styling helped set the overall look of each of these iconic films. Mary eventually left the studio and illustrated children's books, worked as an art director and designed theatrical sets. In 1963 Walt needed help creating a children's pavilion at the 1964–65 New York World's Fair that celebrated children around the world. He knew just who to ask. Mary designed the now-iconic 'It's a Small World' ride. It was so popular, Walt had it replicated in his California theme park, Disneyland. Although it's a Disney fixture, the design is totally Mary and a lasting monument to her style.

Soft-spoken and mild natured, Mary probably never set out to become a legend – but to many in the fields of art, animation, illustration and design, she is legendary.

Chien-Shiung Wu
1912–1997

PHYSICIST
CHINA, USA

Born in a tiny town in China, Chien-Shiung travelled great distances to receive an education. Although it was uncommon at the time, her mother, a teacher, and her father, an engineer, believed their daughter deserved to study just like her two brothers. Their village had no school for girls, so her parents founded one. She soon attended boarding school, then travelled to the university in Nanjing and later all the way to the United States.

In 1936 she enrolled at the University of California, Berkeley, and after receiving her PhD in physics, moved to the East Coast, eventually taking a job at Princeton University. Her research made her a prime candidate to join the Manhattan Project at Columbia University – the US government's secret programme during the Second World War to build the atomic bomb. She was one of only a handful of women and the only Asian American to work on the historic project.

After the war she stayed at Columbia, and in 1956 two male colleagues approached her with an idea: the law of conservation of parity suggested that all subatomic particles decay symmetrically. They believed this wasn't always true, but since they were *theoretical* physicists, they needed Chien-Shiung to conduct an *actual* experiment. She knew this could be a groundbreaking discovery and skipped what would've been her first return trip to China to work on it. The Wu Experiment, as it became known, proved her colleagues' theory.

Her male colleagues received the Nobel Prize in Physics. Chien-Shiung was left out. In 1975, though, she was awarded the National Medal of Science. She was the first woman elected president of the American Physical Society and is recognized today as one of the world's leading experimental physicists. Her book *Beta Decay* is a standard reference text in the field of nuclear physics.

Bessie Blount Griffin
1914–2009

PHYSICAL THERAPIST, INVENTOR
UNITED STATES OF AMERICA

Bessie didn't have an easy childhood but grew up bright, innovative and resilient. At school she was scolded for writing with her left hand. Instead of getting upset, she not only learned to write with her right hand but taught herself to write with her feet as well as her teeth! She made the most out of a difficult situation – and it wouldn't be the last time.

From an early age Bessie wanted to help people, so at college she studied nursing and physical therapy. At the end of the Second World War she volunteered with the Red Cross to work with injured soldiers. She was so good with the soldiers, they called her 'Wonder Woman'! She showed those who couldn't use their hands how to write with their feet or teeth, as she had when she was a child.

She had many ideas for inventions to help her patients become self-sufficient. One idea was a feeding tube that allowed them control over their own eating: users could bite down to release a piece of food to be delivered to an attached spoon! Bessie built her device with simple supplies (plastic, hot water, a hammer) and received a patent. She offered it to the US Veterans Administration, but they were not interested, so she donated it to the French government. She wanted people to know 'that a black woman can invent something for the benefit of humankind.'

Bessie later worked as a forensic scientist, examining handwriting for law enforcement, and in 1977 she trained at the famous Scotland Yard in London, where officers fondly called her 'Mom Bessie'. She opened her own business, examining and preserving pre-Civil War slave documents, and worked towards opening a museum.

In her long life Bessie achieved many things, but helping others was always her goal. She worked into her eighties, determined to leave a legacy and preserve history to share with future generations.

Patent 2,550,554

Fig. 1.

Fig. 3

Fig. 2

Fig. 4.

Fig. 5.

Fig. 6.

Hedy Lamarr
1914 – 2000

ACTRESS, INVENTOR
AUSTRIA, USA

Growing up in Vienna, Austria, curious and creative Hedy (short for Hedwig) loved to go on long walks with her father. He would explain how things worked: everything from the printing press to the tram. As a teenager, Hedy attracted attention for her beauty, and she began to act in films. She married young, but it was an unhappy relationship – her husband was associated with the Nazis and was very controlling. As tensions rose before the Second World War, Hedy escaped both the Nazis and her husband. Careful to keep her Jewish heritage a secret, she rebranded herself as the glamorous Hedy Lamarr and set off for Hollywood – starring in movies such as *Algiers* (1938), which made her an instant star, and the blockbuster *Samson and Delilah* (1949).

During the Second World War the US military was seeking ideas for defensive devices and ways to send messages without any interceptions. Hedy, who was always working on her own projects and inventions, did not want to sit back and make movies while war was raging. She had learned about radio signals from her ex-husband, particularly how they could be blocked. She had an idea for a device that would send signals that hopped across multiple frequencies during transmission, like changing the tune in the middle of a song. It would make a code unbreakable. A composer friend, George Antheil, helped her design it. Although their invention was not used in the war, it was the basis for crucial technology behind wireless signals used for GPS, Bluetooth and Wi-Fi.

Their patent for the 'secret communications system' ran out long before mobile phones came along, so Hedy and George never received major credit, but decades later they received the Electronic Frontier Foundation Pioneer Award, and Hedy became the first woman to win the BULBIE award – also known as the 'Oscar of Inventing'.

Claudia Jones
1915–1964

ACTIVIST, JOURNALIST
TRINIDAD, USA, UK

Born on the Caribbean island of Trinidad, Claudia moved with her family to New York City when she was a child. They'd hoped to find job opportunities, but the United States in the 1920s offered little advancement for people of colour. Instead, they found poor working and living conditions, as well as discrimination. Although she was young, Claudia decided to fight injustice and began to write for local publications.

Claudia discovered the Communist Party USA, which was active in campaigning against segregation. At eighteen, she joined and worked as a journalist, organizer and recruiter. By 1941 the Federal Bureau of Investigation (FBI) was keeping a close eye on anyone associated with communism – an ideology they labelled as un-American. Considered a troublemaker, Claudia was eventually deported to the United Kingdom.

In London Claudia faced the same kind of hostility and discrimination as she did in the United States. She began her activism again, advocating for equal rights for the growing Caribbean immigrant population. Returning to journalism, Claudia founded the *West Indian Gazette*, the United Kingdom's first weekly black newspaper.

After race riots broke out in Notting Hill in 1958, Claudia saw the need to unify her community. Perhaps a carnival, a Caribbean festival and celebration with calypso music and dancing, might help wash away the aftermath of the riots. Claudia was instrumental in organizing it. The first Carnival in London was held in January 1959. It was a precursor to today's Notting Hill Carnival – the biggest Caribbean cultural celebration outside the Caribbean.

Claudia had a vision for the future that was just out of reach and used what she had to advance her fight: her words. Her efforts broke ground for the Civil Rights Movement of the 1960s and made way for the advancement of women, people of colour, and immigrants in two of the most influential countries in the world.

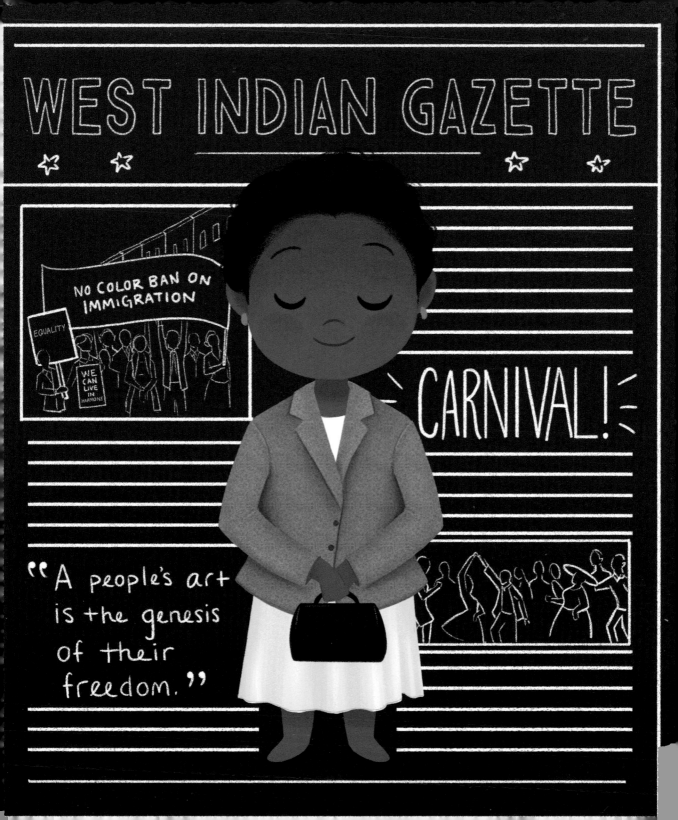

Sister Rosetta Tharpe
1915 – 1973

MUSICIAN
UNITED STATES OF AMERICA

It's hard to say if there was a time in Rosetta's life when she wasn't making music. By the age of six she was already performing in front of a crowd. Her mother was a gospel singer and a preacher, and together they led praise services all around the country. Rosetta was hailed as 'a singing and guitar-playing miracle'. This was hardly an overstatement. It was rare to see a black girl playing the guitar – then considered a man's instrument – and Rosetta was good. Really good.

When she was older, Rosetta went solo, taking gospel music to places it had never been heard before. In 1938 she moved to New York City and signed a landmark deal with Decca Records. She was the first gospel artist at a label famous for jazz and blues musicians such as Louis Armstrong and Billie Holiday. Rosetta bridged the worlds of religious and secular music, performing at nightclubs with some of the most famous musicians around. She wowed audiences with her guitar skills, innovative techniques and energetic songs.

While there is no official first 'rock and roll' song, Rosetta's 1938 hit 'Rock Me' was one of the earliest songs described with the term. Her unique prominence in the mainstream and her pioneering use of the newly electrified guitar helped shape the rock-and-roll genre.

Rosetta's time in the spotlight didn't last long. She was overlooked in the history of music until 2018, when she was inducted into the Rock & Roll Hall of Fame. With her groundbreaking career, she paved the way for artists such as Elvis Presley, Little Richard and Johnny Cash. In a genre of music usually associated with men, Rosetta was a trailblazer and will forever be celebrated as the Godmother of Rock and Roll.

Asima Chatterjee
1917–2006

ORGANIC CHEMIST
INDIA

When Asima was young, her father, a medical doctor, shared with her the fascinating medicinal properties of plants. Encouraged to pursue an education, she studied chemistry at college. Soon after graduating with honours from the University of Calcutta, she began teaching at the nearby Lady Brabourne College. There was no chemistry department at the time, so Asima founded one and became the head of it! In 1944 she completed another degree, becoming the first woman to earn a doctorate in science from an Indian university.

India has a long history of using plants for medical purposes. As technology advanced, scientists were able to extract chemical compounds from the plants and understand what made them work. Asima was at the forefront of this research. There were no fancy machines to help her out. Her work required extreme precision and involved lots of trial and error. But even though it was slow-going, she persisted.

In her research Asima focused exclusively on plants indigenous to India. Among her many successes was an anti-epilepsy drug developed from the dwarf water clover (*Marsilea minuta*), a tiny plant that is often used at the bottom of fish tanks. Who knew something so simple could be so powerful! Asima's research also helped develop an anti-malarial drug from local trees and flowers.

Her lifelong passion was researching alkaloids, such as the vinca alkaloids found in the Madagascar periwinkle (a plant with bright pink flowers). They were found to slow down the multiplication of cancer cells – and are now used in chemotherapy treatments. For her work, Asima received many awards. In 1975 she became the first woman appointed general president of the Indian Science Congress. Asima's discoveries prove that life-changing things can come from just about anywhere – including a flower! Her work has been wildly influential in her field, and her role as a teacher has inspired countless young people to pursue chemistry.

Catharanthus
Roseus

Marsilia
Minuta

Maya Deren
1917–1961

FILM-MAKER
UKRAINE, USA

Maya was always searching for a way to express herself. At college she studied journalism and literature, and in her free time she wrote poetry and stories. When she was hired as the personal assistant to dancer and choreographer Katherine Dunham, Maya became intrigued by dance as expression. She travelled with Dunham's dance troupe, and in Los Angeles she met her future husband, who introduced her to avant-garde cinema.

Maya realized cinema could bring together all the things she was interested in: striking imagery, story, choreography and rhythm. It was the medium she had been waiting for, so she used it to create a visual version of the poetry she was writing. In 1943 she collaborated with her husband to make the landmark experimental short film *Meshes of the Afternoon*. Editing became her most powerful tool – it was a way to mix together images to convey emotion just like the words in her poems. She could use editing to manipulate time and space and create choreography that could not exist in a photograph or a dance performance or a poem.

Maya edited her short film *At Land* like a visual jigsaw puzzle, cutting from scene to scene to show her protagonist (Maya herself) performing an apparently seamless action. In one shot she's climbing a tree; in the next, climbing on to a dinner table.

In 1946 she became the first film-maker to be awarded an esteemed Guggenheim Fellowship. Though she completed only a handful of short films, they were all groundbreaking in the way they conveyed meaning through cinematic techniques.

Maya made films that were artistic and poetic and deeply personal. She helped create a space in the art world for artists who work with cinema and laid the groundwork for the genre of experimental film that has inspired countless creators around the world.

Amalia Hernández
1917–2000

DANCER, CHOREOGRAPHER
MEXICO

From an early age Amalia loved to dance. Her parents were so supportive, they even built her a studio in their home so that she could practise! She was dedicated and disciplined, studying traditional formal ballet. At college she trained in modern dance with European instructors and later worked as a choreographer.

Something was missing, though. Amalia was growing tired of European styles of dance. She was inspired by childhood memories of men and women dancing in the streets in small neighbourhoods and villages in Mexico. These danzas are traditionally used for ceremonial purposes, and they are full of rhythm and energy. Amalia had an idea to combine the uniquely Mexican vibe of the danzas with ballet and modern dance to celebrate her culture.

She started in 1952 with a small group of eight dancers, performing with elaborate costumes, dramatic lighting and creative set designs. Audiences all around Mexico loved it! In 1954 the group began to appear on TV – every week for sixty weeks. Amalia worked hard to create a brand-new performance every week. By 1959 the group, now called Ballet Folklórico de México, had grown to more than fifty dancers, and was so popular that it represented Mexico and performed at the Pan American Games in Chicago.

Over the years Amalia choreographed more than forty ballets, which were performed all over the world. She did extensive research for the performances and took special care to capture the unique footwork and skirt movements of the danzas. She incorporated traditions from more than sixty regions across Mexico.

Some critics accused Amalia of appropriating the traditional danzas for show business, but she was interested in the interpretation of the danzas to celebrate and preserve her culture. Not only did she ignite passion for her Mexican heritage among her people, but she became a cultural ambassador, showcasing Mexico's history around the world!

Violeta Parra
1917–1967

MUSICIAN, ETHNOMUSICOLOGIST
CHILE

Violeta's musical career began at the age of nine. Her father, a music teacher, taught his large family how to sing and play guitar. Together, they toured Chile performing popular songs.

However, Violeta became interested in the country's traditional folk songs, which were in danger of being forgotten. In 1952 she embarked on a life-changing journey to rural villages, meeting with as many elders as she could find and documenting as many folk songs as she could hear. These songs had never been recorded or written down, and Violeta logged more than three thousand of them. She was preserving history and making history at the same time.

Violeta's own music changed in response. She became a pioneer of Nueva Canción, or 'New Song'. This movement used the form of traditional folk song but blended it with contemporary perspectives. In particular, Violeta sang about human rights and the gap between the wealthy and the poor.

Violeta gained recognition throughout Chile and beyond. By 1954 she was performing across Europe, and eventually her recordings sold around the world. Her original songs were a hit, too. Her renowned single 'Gracias a la Vida' ('Thanks to Life') is still one of the most performed and recorded Latin American songs in the world.

Violeta was also a talented painter, embroiderer and ceramicist. She even exhibited her large embroidered tapestries at the Louvre Museum in Paris – becoming the first Latin American artist to have a solo exhibition there.

No matter what she was creating, Violeta's singular goal was to preserve Chilean culture. Today, as Violeta's songs are still being sung and recorded by a new generation of artists, she is celebrated as the mother of Latin American folk music.

Sister Corita Kent
1918–1986

ARTIST, EDUCATOR
UNITED STATES OF AMERICA

Like any young artist, Frances Kent loved to draw, read and make things. But Frances also came from a very religious family, and from a young age she knew she wanted to become a nun. At eighteen, she entered the Roman Catholic religious order at the Immaculate Heart of Mary in Los Angeles. All sisters chose a new name that included *Mary*, so she chose Sister Mary Corita and became known simply as Corita, which means 'little heart'. But there was nothing little about the amount of beauty and love she wanted to share with the world.

She earned her undergraduate degree at Immaculate Heart College and took art classes at the nearby Otis Art Institute and the Chouinard Art Institute. Later, she earned her master's degree in art history and began teaching art at Immaculate Heart, often challenging her students in her popular classes with unexpected assignments.

In her early days, Corita used mainly watercolours and focused on religious subject matter. But after she saw the artist Andy Warhol's famous *Campbell's Soup Cans*, she was inspired to approach her work in a more pop-art style. While Warhol's work was seen as a comment on consumerism, Corita was interested in using mass-market imagery as a way to reach people with her messages of love and compassion. She made posters using popular brands such as Wonder Bread as symbols of the wonder of the Gospel.

In the 1960s her work became more political as the Civil Rights Movement and the war in Vietnam shook up the United States. From images of Martin Luther King Jr to verses from the Bible, Corita used her art to draw attention to social injustices around the world.

In her long career she created hundreds of prints and thousands of watercolours. Corita was best known for her serigraphs: a type of silkscreen print. She created bold, graphic images – perfect for sending her bold messages of love and peace.

Esther Afua Ocloo
1919 – 2002

ENTREPRENEUR
GHANA

Although Esther came from an underprivileged family in what was then the British colony of the Gold Coast, she grew up learning farming and trade skills that would one day lead her to great success. With her family's encouragement and a scholarship, Esther attended a prestigious school in the capital, Accra. After graduation she needed to make money to support herself. Her aunt had given her ten shillings – less than one US dollar – but through determination and skill, Esther turned it into much more.

With six of her shillings, she bought supplies (sugar, oranges, used jars, and firewood for cooking) and developed her own marmalade recipe. She sold each jar for one shilling, earning back her money with a profit! Her plan worked out even better than expected: she was offered a contract to provide juice and marmalade to her old school and later another contract with the military. Esther couldn't maintain production by herself, so she secured a bank loan to grow her business. In 1942 she opened the first food-processing plant in Ghana: Nkulenu Industries. (It still ships marmalade and other food products all around the world.)

To develop her food science and cooking skills, Esther went to study in England. When she returned home in the 1950s, around the time Ghana declared independence, she worked hard to help her country grow. Remembering the impact her loan had had on her business, she wanted to help local women improve their lives as well as contribute to the economy. In 1976, along with Michaela Walsh and Ela Bhatt, she founded Women's World Banking (WWB), a non-profit organization that works with financial institutions to provide micro-loans, small loans with low interest, for women who need help to grow a small business. WWB has given out millions of dollars in loans and has helped more than thirty million women around the world. In 1990 Esther was awarded the Africa Prize for Leadership – the first woman to win – and she is celebrated as a pioneer and advocate for women!

Monir Shahroudy Farmanfarmaian
1924–

VISUAL ARTIST
IRAN, USA

As a child, Monir didn't consider herself an artist. She learned to draw from copying postcards of famous paintings, just to pass the time. Her art tutor was impressed with her skill, though, and urged her to keep working at it. Monir had never received encouragement like that before, and soon she was hooked!

She studied art at the University of Tehran and in 1945 went to art school in New York City, where she visited museums and saw the paintings she knew only from postcards.

In 1957 Monir returned to Iran with a fresh outlook. She was filled with new-found respect for her country's traditional art forms: architecture, reverse glass painting and Turkoman jewellery. Visiting the Shah Cheragh (King of the Light) Mosque in Shiraz was a major turning point in her career. Like many mosques, it features elaborate geometric forms, a domed ceiling and elegant ornaments, but the Shah Cheragh also has thousands of tiny mirrors in its tile work. The walls glisten and gleam as they reflect the environment and people. Astounded by its beauty, and believing there were infinite possibilities in the geometry, Monir was inspired to take the mirrors into the world and reflect life in Iran. Some of her most famous pieces were mirrored balls – many people mistook them for disco balls, but she had actually been inspired by children playing with a football in Tehran. She wanted to create a mirrored mosaic on the surface of an object that represented youth and light.

Monir spent more than twenty years in exile in the United States, unable to return to Iran after a political and religious revolution started there in 1979. Much of her work and her personal collection had been confiscated or destroyed. She finally made it home in 2004. In Tehran, she continues to make art, and there's a museum dedicated to her body of work. It took a long time, but now, in her nineties, Monir is celebrated as a visionary artist for her ability to see story and culture in elegant geometry.

46

Mahasweta Devi
1926–2016

WRITER, ACTIVIST
INDIA

Mahasweta was born into a large family in India's Bengal region when the country was still under British rule. Her father was a poet, her uncle was a film-maker, and her mother was a writer and social worker. Though she grew up firmly middle class, nearly everyone in her family dedicated their work to helping India's poor and marginalized. It wasn't long before Mahasweta would do the same.

Mahasweta began writing at the age of thirteen. In her early days she wrote love stories but never showed them to anyone! At the University of Calcutta she studied English, and later she became a professor and worked as a reporter.

At thirty, Mahasweta published her first novel, *The Queen of Jhansi* — inspired by the true story of a nineteenth-century queen turned warrior. She travelled all across northern India, talking with villagers and listening to their versions of the Jhansi legend. She wanted to capture what the story meant to them, as they had passed it down from generation to generation.

At the time, Bengali literature focused mostly on the middle class, so it was radical for Mahasweta to shine a literary light on India's poor and disenfranchised. She was particularly passionate about telling the stories of India's indigenous peoples, many of whom had been demonized by the Criminal Tribes Act. Once, a young tribal girl told her that in school they learned about Indian heroes and other figures, and she asked, 'Did we have no heroes?' This solidified for Mahasweta why it was important to share those stories: to give a voice to the voiceless and offer representation to those without it.

She wrote more than a hundred novels and twenty collections of short stories. She was given countless awards but never felt any of them reached her heart as the people did. Mahasweta used her platform to comment on injustice, inequality and women's rights and worked hard to help all those around her.

Vera Rubin
1928–2016

ASTRONOMER
UNITED STATES OF AMERICA

Vera was always good at asking questions, often about the stars in the sky. She used to stare out of her window at night, charting their movements. Vera didn't just think the moon was pretty; she wondered why it looked like it followed her when her family drove in the car.

Inspired by the pioneering nineteenth-century American astronomer Maria Mitchell, and despite being discouraged by her high-school science teacher, Vera decided to study the stars – and she would do it where Maria Mitchell taught: Vassar College. After graduating from Vassar as the only astronomy major in 1948, she wanted to apply to Princeton's graduate programme, but she was turned away because they didn't accept women.

Vera didn't let that deter her. She continued her education elsewhere, and she kept asking questions no one else was asking. She always wanted to know what she didn't know, and that would soon lead her to make one of astronomy's greatest discoveries.

In the 1970s, she and a colleague who had been studying the behaviour of spiral galaxies noticed that the stars at the edge of a galaxy were moving just as fast as the ones in the middle. This didn't follow Newton's Theory of Gravitation; based on its calculations, objects further away from the galaxy's centre should have been moving more slowly. Vera reasoned that there must be something we cannot see affecting the gravity. Luminous matter is the name for the objects we can see in the night sky – such as planets and stars. In the 1930s, the astronomer Fritz Zwicky had speculated about the existence of matter we cannot see: dark matter. Vera's observations helped to prove its existence. We now believe that a lot of our universe is made up of dark matter – one more step towards understanding the cosmos!

Yayoi Kusama
1929–

ARTIST

JAPAN, USA

Art was always a way for Yayoi to express herself. But her parents did not approve of art as a career. Yayoi, however, could not be stopped. Even when her mother took her drawing tools away, she made her own. Eventually she convinced her family to allow her to study traditional art. However, she soon grew tired of the conservative style of painting and became increasingly interested in the abstract expressionism movement in the Western art world. In 1958 she moved to New York City, where she worked on paintings, made sculptures and shot films. Some of her most famous artistic successes, though, were her happenings – art events and performances conducted around the city.

Yayoi's work is unique and recognizable for her frequent use of bright polka dots and repeating patterns. Much of her creative process is marked by her focus and fixations. She's known for creating hundreds of paintings in a single series and filling those paintings with thousands of dots. The continuous patterns cover her canvases so that the final work is without composition, without beginning or end. She used dots as symbolism for humanity and existence: to her, humans are just dots on the earth, which is just a dot in a universe filled with billions of other dots, on and on into infinity. She carried this idea into her immersive installations that she called 'infinity rooms'. They are mirrored rooms that create the illusion of looking into infinity. She decorates them with different objects she's created: sometimes shiny balls, decorated pumpkins, or more polka dots. These spaces create a unique experience for the viewer, as they feel simultaneously enclosed and expansive.

In 1973 Yayoi returned to her home country of Japan and launched a successful literary career. Now in her eighties, Yayoi has gained another wave of success with her infinity rooms popping up all over the world and on social media! With a career that spans seven decades, Yayoi forged a path where there was none.

Toni Morrison
1931–

WRITER
UNITED STATES OF AMERICA

Toni grew up among storytellers. Her parents and grandparents shared folktales and ghost stories and sang songs every evening. Toni always begged to hear her favourites, and when she knew the endings, she made up new ones. This kind of family storytelling is part of a long tradition in African American culture. It helped instil a great sense of pride in her heritage and was a huge influence on Toni's writing.

Among Toni's favourite authors were Jane Austen and Leo Tolstoy. In the work of the Russian master Tolstoy she found encouragement to write about her own community and experiences. His stories focused on his culture and she was reading it, so why couldn't others read about hers?

For a while Toni dedicated her life to other people's writing, as a college professor and as an editor for the publisher Random House, where she championed writers of colour.

At thirty-nine, she published her first novel, *The Bluest Eye*, the story of a black girl who feels ugly and unimportant and believes her life would be better if she had blue eyes. Toni used her stories to address the realities of the African American experience and in her debut called out issues of identity and problematic beauty standards.

She went on to write ten more novels. Whether set in the past or present, Toni's stories reflect the histories of America, often with magic, myth and fantasy woven in.

Her fifth novel, *Beloved*, earned Toni the highest literary award in America, the Pulitzer Prize for Fiction. In 1993 she received the Nobel Prize in Literature for her body of work, becoming the first black woman in the world to win it.

Beyond the awards and accolades, her lasting legacy will be the countless readers and writers she's inspired. Whether it's through her teaching, editing or writing, Toni's love for storytelling has changed American literature forever.

Esther Mahlangu
1935 –

PAINTER
SOUTH AFRICA

When Esther learned to paint at the age of ten, it was hard to get her to stop. She was born in the southern Ndebele tribe of South Africa. In her culture it is a tradition for women to paint the exterior walls of their homes in patterns that celebrate their ancestry and heritage. Mothers pass down the skill to their daughters, who paint their homes when they marry. But Esther could not wait! Her mother gave her a small spot at the back of her house to practise the bold and colourful geometric patterns found in her culture's clothing and jewellery.

As an adult, Esther lived and worked in the Botshabelo Historical Village, a museum of Ndebele culture and heritage. In 1986 art researchers from Paris met Esther and invited her to participate in *Magicians of the World* – a landmark exhibition dedicated to showcasing traditional artists from around the world. It was her breakthrough moment, and it put the Ndebele culture on a global stage.

Soon Esther was being commissioned to share her art all over the world, including painting murals in New York and Johannesburg. Her work was even featured on a British Airways aeroplane, a landmark moment for African art!

Traditionally, Esther painted with colours made from plants and clay from the forests and rivers of her native land (reds, browns, yellows, as well as black and white), but over the years she has incorporated contemporary commercial paints into her palette, such as bright pinks and neons. The result is unique and colourful – like Esther herself.

She is passionate about sharing her knowledge with a younger generation as part of her mission to keep Ndebele customs alive. Esther dreams of formal schools and other facilities that teach African art. Meanwhile, Esther took it upon herself to open a school in her own back yard, in Mthambothini, to teach any who want to learn.

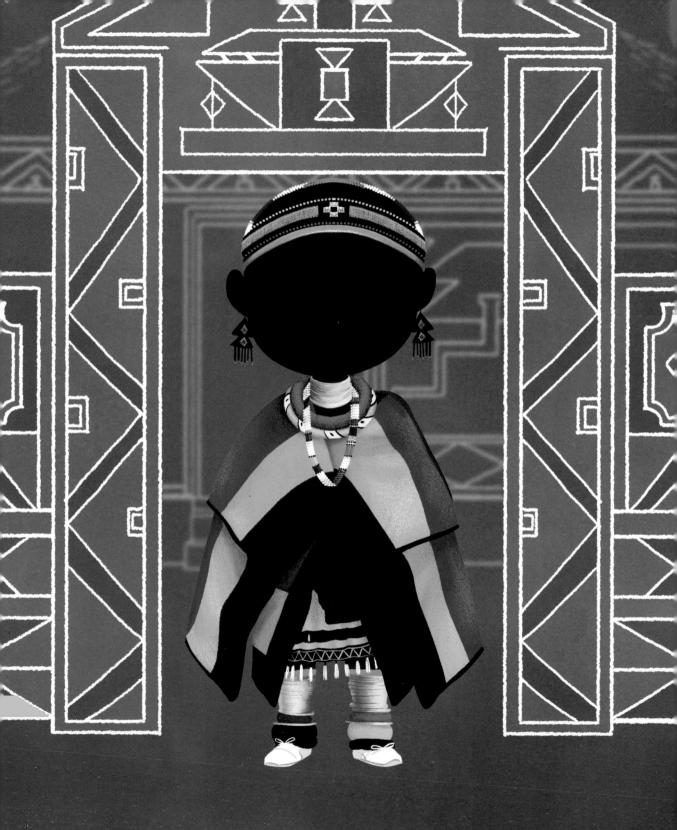

Thancoupie Gloria Fletcher
1937–2011

CERAMICIST, VISUAL ARTIST
AUSTRALIA

Thancoupie grew up in a tight Aboriginal community in a mission town near Weipa, Queensland, Australia. When she was young everyone from the various tribes lived together, speaking different languages, including hers, Thaynakwith. The female elders passed down tradition, stories and legends and taught their unique symbols by drawing in the sand. This is where Thancoupie fell in love with art.

Although she was shy, Thancoupie dedicated herself to educating the young as well as to making traditional art. In her mid-thirties she shocked everyone by announcing she was leaving to study art in Sydney, one of the biggest cities in Australia.

Although she intended to study painting, Thancoupie ended up in the ceramics studio. In Weipa, clay was sacred, to be used only as body paint for ceremonial purposes, and it was not to be touched by children. Even as an adult, Thancoupie was hesitant to break the rules, but also a little bit excited! With pottery, she could celebrate her culture. In her signature bowls and spheres, she used intricate patterns and symbols to trace the stories of her people, etching history on their surfaces. Her clay sculptures have been exhibited around the world, and shy Thancoupie became one of Australia's greatest artists.

When she returned home, she could see the community changing. The older people were dying, and with them their culture and customs. By the time she became a primary elder, Thancoupie was the last fluent speaker of the Thaynakwith language. In an effort to preserve it, she worked for ten years recording audio and writing down stories to create *Thanakupi's Guide to Language & Culture: A Thaynakwith Dictionary*.

One of her goals was to instil a sense of cultural pride in the younger generation. She mentored young artists and founded the Weipa Festival to teach children the traditional songs, dances and language.

Eiko Ishioka
1938–2012

ART DIRECTOR, PRODUCTION DESIGNER
JAPAN

By the time Eiko was seven, she knew she wanted to follow in her father's footsteps and become a graphic designer. At the time, though, design was a career strictly for men. Although her father warned her against it, he didn't stop her from trying because he knew Eiko was born to go against the grain.

At college her male peers didn't believe she could be successful, and even when she won one of Japan's biggest awards in advertising, they undercut her success by claiming she won only *because* she was a woman. From that day, Eiko vowed to work hard to prove them wrong. She adopted a mantra: Timeless, Revolutionary, Original. Everything she created would have to live up to those standards.

In her twenty years in advertising Eiko was a powerhouse! Her unique aesthetic was unmistakable, and she was soon considered Japan's foremost art director. Because she had more creativity to offer and more barriers to break, she switched fields and began to work in production design, creating elaborate sets for movies and plays.

Then she tried something totally new: costume design. American film-maker Francis Ford Coppola hired her to create costumes for his adaptation of Bram Stoker's classic novel *Dracula.* Eiko created designs that were pure outward expressions of the creepy darkness of the story. The final products were so striking that they are typically the first thing associated with the film. For her incredible work, Eiko was awarded an Academy Award in 1993!

Eiko went on to create costumes for the likes of Björk, Grace Jones, Julie Taymor, Tarsem Singh and Cirque du Soleil – creatives known for their unique, avant-garde styles. They pushed the boundaries of beauty, and Eiko helped bring those ideas to the forefront through costume and design. Her many awards do little to showcase how big an impact she's had on the world of design, not only for women but for anyone who likes to go against the grain!

Wangari Maathai
1940–2011

ENVIRONMENTALIST, ACTIVIST
KENYA

Wangari was born in the Kenyan village of Ihithe. Her parents were farmers and members of the Anjiru clan of the Kikuyu. Each clan is marked by a unique trade or gift; Wangari's is known for its leadership. Her people had a strong connection to the land, and in Wangari's youth it was lush and fertile, food was abundant and seasons changed like clockwork.

But the country was changing. Over-cultivation and deforestation ravaged the landscape, and revolution was on the horizon. Kenya was under longtime British rule, but in the 1950s the Mau Mau rebellion, led by a large coalition of freedom fighters, began.

Meanwhile, encouraged by a teacher in high school, Wangari developed a love for science. She earned her undergraduate degree in biological sciences, and her master's degree, in the United States. At the University of Nairobi, in 1971, she became the first woman in either east or central Africa to earn a doctorate.

She served on the National Council of Women of Kenya, whose goal was to support and unite the many groups around the country – especially as the newly independent Kenya was taking shape. There, she proposed that women should plant trees, both to conserve the environment and to improve their quality of life. She expanded this idea to create the Green Belt Movement, which spread to many other countries. Wangari helped women plant more than twenty million trees on farms and at schools and church compounds, a project that ensured fuel for cooking and a more nutritious diet.

In 2004 Wangari received the Nobel Peace Prize 'for her contribution to sustainable development, democracy and peace'. Wangari was also a member of the Parliament of Kenya, advocating for human rights and women's rights. Wangari believed that a positive attitude and trust in people's inherent goodness were essential to making change. She was a fierce fighter and leader for democracy, human rights and environmental conservation.

Calypso Rose
1940–

CALYPSO SINGER
TRINIDAD AND TOBAGO

McCartha Linda Sandy Lewis was born on Tobago – the smaller of the two islands that make up the Republic of Trinidad and Tobago. Although a tiny nation in the Caribbean, it has had a huge impact on the world of music as the birthplace of calypso. With strong folkloric roots, calypso music has always reflected the people's lives and struggles, but it is defined by its upbeat rhythm and vibe. Every year in the Caribbean, the music and dance celebration known as Carnival takes place. This is where Rose made her name.

Despite growing up with a pronounced stutter and a father who did not approve of the Carnival scene, Rose was drawn to it. In 1955, at the age of fifteen, Rose wrote her first song, 'Glass Thief'. Inspired by real events, it was one of the first calypso songs to focus on the unjust treatment of women.

Calypso had long been defined by its most famous male performers, and many made their name by winning the biggest competition around: the Calypso King, held at the annual Carnival celebrations. In 1963 Rose entered the competition, performed her hit song 'Cooperation', and won the title of Calypso King for the year! No woman had ever won, so the title had never been considered exclusionary. A few years later Rose won again . . . and again. In 1978 the organizers of Carnival changed the name to Calypso Monarch, paving the way for more girls to enter the competition!

Rose's name has become synonymous with calypso. She has written more than eight hundred songs and has recorded more than twenty albums. All along her journey, she has broken down barriers and defied expectations, and she has been widely recognized for bringing a strong female perspective into the world of calypso and using her music as a voice for women in the Caribbean.

Flossie Wong-Staal
1947–

VIROLOGIST, MOLECULAR BIOLOGIST
CHINA, HONG KONG, USA

Born Wong Yee Ching in China, Flossie fled the Communist Revolution with her family when she was five years old and settled in what was then the British colony of Hong Kong. At her Catholic school, the teachers encouraged her family to take English names. For Yee Ching, her father chose Flossie, the name of a recent typhoon. Maybe he knew that one day his daughter would be a force to be reckoned with!

At high school students had to choose a course of study: science or the humanities. Flossie was interested in literature and poetry, but she chose science and never looked back. She studied biology and microbiology in the USA. In the 1960s and 1970s, many molecular discoveries were made, and it was an exciting time to be in that field. Flossie was part of a wave of young researchers hoping to make the next big discovery that could help the world.

In 1973 she began working on viruses at the National Cancer Institute. In the early 1980s a new disease was spreading, like nothing doctors had ever seen: unusual infections in some patients and aggressive cancers in others. It was called acquired immune deficiency syndrome (AIDS). Within a year of the first case being discovered, more than one hundred people had already died from it. The clock was ticking to figure out what was causing it.

Scientists determined it had to be a virus, and in 1983 Flossie and her team identified HIV – the human immunodeficiency virus – as the cause of AIDS. The first step towards a solution is identifying the problem, so this was a landmark discovery! Over the next two years Flossie worked to help develop a test to see if someone was carrying the virus and to find a treatment. She is one of the leading scientists in the world on this subject.

Flossie has developed more than forty tests, procedures and inventions relating to HIV, AIDS and other illnesses, proving that inventing and discovering don't have to look big to be impressive – even something microscopic can change the world!

66

Zaha Hadid
1950–2016

ARCHITECT
IRAQ, UK

At eleven years old, Zaha knew she wanted to design buildings. Her mother let her prove her skill by decorating some rooms in the house. It's safe to say that, even as a child, Zaha had impeccable taste. Born in Baghdad, Iraq, Zaha studied maths at the American University of Beirut, in Lebanon, before heading to London to study architecture.

In architecture school, Zaha followed the rules her first few years, but for her final project she let loose. She was inspired by the work of the Russian abstract painter Kazimir Malevich and re-envisioned one of his works as a three-dimensional building. By graduation, she had made a huge impact at the school with her imaginative designs and futuristic ideas.

In 1979 she opened her own architecture firm in London. Zaha became known for her dynamic sculptural forms, often using curving shapes that swept through space and flowed like water. Her bold approach to architecture brought her attention and won competitions. However, many of her designs were criticized as too avant-garde and impractical to ever get made. Sometimes she was called the 'paper architect' because her designs rarely moved past the sketch phase. But soon the world caught on to Zaha's vision.

Some of her notable buildings include the London Aquatics Centre, designed for the 2012 Olympics, and the MAXXI National Museum of 21st Century Arts in Rome; she also received the Pritzker Architecture Prize – and became the first woman to receive the field's most prestigious award. She was made Dame Commander of the British Empire for her contributions to architecture.

At the time of her death at the age of sixty-five, she was considered one of the world's greatest architects. Her firm continues her vision without her, completing many of the projects she had in the works. Her elegant buildings stand as her lasting legacy to the world.

Maya Lin
1959–

SCULPTOR, ARCHITECT
UNITED STATES OF AMERICA

Growing up in Athens, Ohio, Maya lived in a house surrounded by woods. She played outside, feeding birds, trying to tame rabbits and exploring the hills – she nicknamed her favourite 'the lizard's back'. Maya was the daughter of a ceramicist and a poet, and her creative thinking was fostered at home.

As she grew older, Maya wanted a career that would combine her passions – nature, mathematics, art and science – so at college she studied architecture. In 1981, during her senior year, she entered a competition to design the Vietnam Veterans Memorial in Washington, DC. Maya had an idea for something simple and elegant: a V-shaped wall, cut into the ground, that featured the approximately 58,000 names of those who died or went missing in the war etched into the polished black granite. She did not want the memorial to be about what anyone thought of the war. She wanted to create a space for reflection and healing. Out of more than 1,400 anonymous entries, Maya's was selected. Everyone was surprised to find out she was a young woman still in college!

Many people were critical of her concept, but it is now one of the most visited monuments in the United States. She went on to design the Civil Rights Memorial in Montgomery, Alabama, and has created many other large-scale artworks around the country. Maya takes special care to be respectful of the environment, often incorporating the earth's natural formations and utilizing renewable resources in her work.

As an artist, architect and committed environmentalist, Maya seeks to make people aware of their surroundings – physically and psychologically. In 2005 she was inducted into the National Women's Hall of Fame, and in 2009 she was awarded the National Medal of Arts. Maya pursues new perspectives and creative ways to celebrate the beauty of the natural world around us.

More *Little Leaders*

There are visionary women all around the world and throughout history, many more than I had the space to showcase in this book. The fields of art and science are vast, so I tried to incorporate as wide a range as possible, from the many categories and specialities as well as various regions and centuries. But of course there are still so many stories to tell.

From the first known novelist to one of the first known female mathematicians, here are a few more thinkers and creators who blazed a trail all their own. If they spark your interest I urge you to learn more about them. Use the Further Reading, Watching and Listening section to find resources to continue your study, either through books, movies or the internet!

Are there some famous names you might include? Maybe someone from another field altogether – an activist, teacher or athlete? A composer, toymaker or chef? Perhaps there's someone whose story has never been told? Or maybe even the story that's in your future? Whichever it may be, I hope the following pages encourage you in your curiosity. Use my sources to delve deeper and conduct your own research. Reference the glossary for terms you may not know.

Get inspired! Try out new things! Ask questions! And be sure to share the amazing things you discover!

HYPATIA OF ALEXANDRIA

circa 370–415

Philosopher, astronomer, mathematician and educator. She was one of the earliest female mathematicians in recorded history and one of the last great thinkers of Alexandria in ancient Egypt.

MURASAKI SHIKIBU

circa 978–1014

Japanese poet, novelist and lady-in-waiting at the imperial court in the Heian period. Celebrated author of *The Tale of Genji*, thought to be the first novel ever written. Her real name is unknown – only her pen name has survived.

ARTEMISIA GENTILESCHI
1593–1653

Italian painter known for her skill in accurately painting the female form and depicting the female point of view. She featured strong women from myths, allegories and the Bible in her work.

MARIA MITCHELL
1818–1889

America's first professional female astronomer and the first American scientist to discover a comet, Miss Mitchell's Comet. She was an advocate for girls in mathematics and science and taught astronomy at Vassar College.

EDMONIA LEWIS
circa 1844–1907

American sculptor whose speciality was portrait busts. She trained in Rome and became the first woman of African American and Native American heritage to achieve international recognition as a sculptor.

EMMY NOETHER
1882–1935

German mathematician who developed an important theory of physics known as Noether's theorem. Albert Einstein and others considered her one of the most important mathematicians of all time.

MARTHA GRAHAM
1894–1991

American dancer and choreographer, known as the Mother of Modern Dance. She created the Graham technique, which emphasizes the human body's potential for expression. She danced and taught for more than seventy years.

URSULA NORDSTROM
1910–1988

American book editor and publisher, responsible for a shift in children's literature towards books appealing directly to children's imaginations. Some of the books she worked on include *Harriet the Spy*, *Where the Wild Things Are*, *Goodnight Moon* and *Charlotte's Web*.

IOLANI LUAHINE
1915–1978

Hawaiian dancer, chanter, and *kumu hula*, a master teacher of the art of hula. She is respected for her knowledge of the sacred ceremony and celebrated for her advocacy and conservation of her culture.

ROSALIND FRANKLIN
1920–1958

British chemist who contributed significant research on the molecular structures of DNA, RNA and viruses. She successfully used X-rays to photograph DNA, leading to the discovery of its double-helix structure.

SHIVANI
1923–2003

One of India's most popular authors.
She was a pioneer of women's fiction
and wrote more than forty novels.
Many of her stories were published
in Hindi-language magazines
specifically for India's population.
Her first story was published
when she was twelve!

CORETTA SCOTT KING
1927–2006

American civil rights activist and the
wife of Martin Luther King Jr. After he
was assassinated in 1968, she played
a prominent role in the Civil Rights
Movement, expanding its reach and
promoting her husband's legacy,
in part by working to establish his
birthday as a national holiday.

MIRIAM MAKEBA
1932–2008

South African singer and activist known as Mama Africa, famous for popularizing Afropop music around the world. She spoke out against apartheid in South Africa (and was exiled for that) and worked as a goodwill ambassador for the United Nations.

BUFFY SAINTE-MARIE
1941–

Canadian musician, artist and activist who uses her work and reputation to focus on issues important to the indigenous peoples of the Americas. Founder of the Cradleboard Teaching Project, which educates children about Native Americans and fosters cross-cultural communication.

SHIRLEY ANN JACKSON
1946–

American physicist, specializing in theoretical physics. She was the first African American woman to earn a PhD from the Massachusetts Institute of Technology and to be awarded the National Medal of Science, and she was active in bringing more diversity to MIT.

CINDY SHERMAN
1954–

American photographer and visual artist known for her conceptual portraits. Recipient of a MacArthur Fellowship (aka the genius grant), she acts as her own model (and make-up artist), using her photos to explore identity and representation, and to subvert stereotypes of women.

OLGA D. GONZÁLEZ-SANABRIA
1955–

Puerto Rican scientist and inventor who developed the long-cycle-life nickel-hydrogen batteries that help power the International Space Station. She was the longtime director of engineering at NASA's John H. Glenn Research Center.

MARYAM MIRZAKHANI
1977–2017

Iranian mathematician, professor at Princeton and then Stanford, and specialist in the geometry of curved surfaces. In 2014 she became the first woman and the first Iranian to win the Fields Medal, the most prestigious award in mathematics.

Further Reading,

WATCHING AND LISTENING

I read a lot of books and articles and watched a lot of documentaries while researching the women in this book – for both the text and the art. Sometimes I had to leave out really cool pieces of their stories. But if you're interested (and I hope you are!), you can use the following resources to learn more about these women and to begin your own research.

SEE THEIR WORK
At Land (1944): Directed by Maya Deren
Mirror Mirror (2012): Costume design by Eiko Ishioka
Roman Holiday (1953): Costume design by Edith Head
Samson and Delilah (1949): Starring Hedy Lamarr, costume design by Edith Head

HEAR THEIR MUSIC
Sister Rosetta Tharpe: 'Strange Things Happening Every Day' (1944)
Violeta Parra: 'Gracias a la Vida' (1966)
Calypso Rose: 'Calypso Queen' (2016)

BOOKS BY LITTLE LEADERS

Edith Head: *The Dress Doctor*

Peggy Guggenheim: *Out of This Century: Confessions of an Art Addict*

Gyo Fujikawa: *Babies*

Mary Blair: *I Can Fly*

Monir Shahroudy Farmanfarmaian: *A Mirror Garden: A Memoir*

Mahasweta Devi: *The Queen of Jhansi*

Vera Rubin: *Bright Galaxies, Dark Matters*

Toni Morrison: *The Bluest Eye*

Thancoupie Gloria Fletcher: *Thanakupi's Guide to Language & Culture:
    A Thaynakwith Dictionary*

Wangari Maathai: *Unbowed: A Memoir*

MOVIES ABOUT LITTLE LEADERS

Bombshell: The Hedy Lamarr Story (2017)

Calypso Rose: The Lioness of the Jungle (2011)

The Godmother of Rock & Roll: Sister Rosetta Tharpe (2011)

Imagine . . .: Toni Morrison Remembers (2015)

Maya Lin: A Strong Clear Vision (1994)

Walt & El Grupo (2008)

WEBSITES FOR RESEARCH

Art21.org	NASA.gov	Stellarium.org
Corita.org	Nobelprize.org	Womensworldbanking.org
Guggenheim.org	Oscars.org	Yayoi-Kusama.jp
Magicofmaryblair.com	Pulitzer.org	Zaha-hadid.com

⊰⊱⊱ SOURCES ⊰⊰⊱

Here are other sources I consulted in my research. Some of the books are not easy to find, but others are readily available. All of them are fascinating.

Aschenbrenner, Joyce. *Katherine Dunham: Dancing a Life.* Urbana: University of Illinois Press, 2002.

Curie, Marie. *Pierre Curie.* 1923. Reprint, Mineola, NY: Dover Publications, 2012.

Davies, Carole Boyce. *Left of Karl Marx: The Political Life of Black Communist Claudia Jones.* Durham, NC: Duke University Press, 2007.

Devi, Mahasweta. *Imaginary Maps: Three Stories.* Translated by Gayatri Chakravorty Spivak. New York: Routledge, 1995.

Godbole, Rohini M., and Ram Ramaswamy, eds. *Lilavati's Daughters: The Women Scientists of India.* Bangalore: Indian Academy of Sciences, 2008.

Hassani, Salim T. S. al-, ed. *1001 Inventions: The Enduring Legacy of Muslim Civilization.* Washington, DC: National Geographic, 2012.

Isaacs, Jennifer, and Thancoupie. *Thancoupie the Potter.* Sydney: Aboriginal Artists Agency, 1982.

Isaacson, Walter. *The Innovators: How a Group of Hackers, Geniuses, and Geeks Created the Digital Revolution.* New York: Simon & Schuster, 2014.

Ishioka, Eiko. *Eiko Ishioka.* Edited by Jianping He. Singapore: Page One Pub, 2006.

Jorgensen, Jay. *Edith Head: The Fifty-year Career of Hollywood's Greatest Costume Designer.* Philadelphia: Running Press, 2010.

Lee, Lily Xiao Hong, and A. D. Stefanowska, eds. *Biographical Dictionary of Chinese Women.* 2 vols. Armonk, NY: M. E. Sharpe, 1998–2003.

Munro, John. *The Anticolonial Front: The African American Freedom Struggle and Global Decolonisation, 1945–1960.* Cambridge: Cambridge University Press, 2017.

Peterson, Barbara Bennett, ed. *Notable Women of China: Shang Dynasty to the Early Twentieth Century.* New York: Routledge, 2015.

Shay, Anthony. *Choreographic Politics: State Folk Dance Companies, Representation, and Power.* Middletown, CT: Wesleyan University Press, 2002.

Stanley, Autumn. *Mothers and Daughters of Invention: Notes for a Revised History of Technology.* New Brunswick, NJ: Rutgers University Press, 1995.

GLOSSARY

ABORIGINAL People, plants or animals native to a region. Aboriginal Australians are people indigenous to mainland Australia or Tasmania.

ABSTRACT Art that isn't grounded in reality.

ABSTRACT EXPRESSIONISM An art movement that emerged during and after the Second World War when artists rejected conventional techniques and created pieces with energetic lines, movement and colour that evoked emotion.

AESTHETIC An individual's theory or set of ideas about what is beautiful: one's personal style or taste.

AFRICAN DIASPORA Migration and resettling of people from Africa around the world.

ALKALOID A chemical compound that contains nitrogen and is often found in plants. Many have medicinal properties and can be used by humans.

ANTHROPOLOGY The study of humans and their societies, cultures and development.

APARTHEID A policy of racial segregation in South Africa, in place from 1948 to 1994. It allowed for discrimination against black, Asian and mixed-race South Africans and promoted a political culture based on white supremacy.

ATOM The smallest unit of matter that still has the properties of a chemical element. Everything, including this book, is made up of billions and billions of atoms.

AVANT-GARDE French for 'advance guard' — referring to part of an army that advances ahead of the group — it is a term used to describe new and unusual or experimental approaches to something, especially the creative process and within the art world.

COBOL Acronym for common business-oriented language, a computer programming language that resembles ordinary English, based on Grace Hopper's FLOW-MATIC programming language. She is often referred to as the 'grandmother of COBOL'.

CRIMINAL TRIBES ACT Legislation enacted in India during British rule (first in 1871) that unjustly characterized people from India's ethnic tribes as criminals and put harsh restrictions on their daily lives.

CUBISM An art movement in the early 1900s created by Pablo Picasso and Georges Braque that embraced geometric shapes and different points of view to explore the two-dimensional nature of canvas.

DARK MATTER The name for non-luminous matter in the universe, associated with gravitational attraction but not directly detectable. We don't know what it is yet, or if it is even 'matter', but some scientists believe about 30 per cent of our universe is made up of this dark stuff that emits no light or energy.

ETHNOGRAPHIC Studying people and their culture by observing their lives.

GUGGENHEIM FELLOWSHIP A prestigious financial grant for scholars and artists to pursue research or study in the arts (established by Simon Guggenheim, uncle of Peggy).

INDUSTRIAL REVOLUTION A rapid change in economy in the eighteenth and nineteenth centuries in Europe and America, sparked by the introduction of new machinery. Much of manufacturing shifted from being done by hand to being done by machines.

MISSION TOWN A town established by Christian missionaries as a religious outpost. Usually they built a church and a school.

NEWTON'S THEORY OF GRAVITATION Isaac Newton's mathematical principle describes the attraction between two objects that have mass, explaining in his theory that gravitational force decreases with distance.

POP ART An art movement that emerged in the 1950s and took inspiration from the bright, bold images from mass media and popular culture: advertisements, comic books, food labels, logos and more.

PRODUCTION DESIGN In movies, TV shows and theatre, the production designer manages the art department and oversees the visual aspect of what is on stage or in front of the camera.

RADIOACTIVITY The energy released when an atom with an unstable nucleus splits (such as in uranium).

ROSENWALD FUND A philanthropic fund created in 1917 for 'the well-being of mankind' and used in large part to improve education for black children in the American rural South.

SPIRAL GALAXY A system of vast numbers of stars, bound together by gravitational forces, that is shaped in a flat, swirly disc with long, spiral 'arms' of stars (as opposed to irregular galaxies, which have no regular shape).

SUBATOMIC PARTICLES Particles smaller than an atom – such as the protons and neutrons found in an atom's nucleus and the electrons that travel around it. Far more kinds have been detected or predicted, including smaller components such as quarks.

SURREALISM An art movement beginning in the 1920s in which painters and artists depicted otherworldly and dreamlike images we often see in our minds or subconscious but not in nature.

TEHUANA Of or relating to Tehuantepec, a city in the Mexican state of Oaxaca. Known for its empowered women and their traditional dress.

VIRUS A tiny infectious agent that replicates itself inside the cells of a living host.

Acknowledgements

Bigger. That's what I wanted. Going into creating this book, I knew I wanted it to be bigger than my first. To feel bigger, packed with stories of incredible people from all around the world. Within minutes of writing the first bio, though, it became clear to me just how big an undertaking this was. There was so much to research, so much to learn, and so much to say. From experimental physics to ninth-century Moroccan clothing, this was a whole other beast entirely. I learned a lot, and found new passions, but I would never have been able to complete this book without the help and support of many thoughtful and talented people.

My editor, Farrin Jacobs, deserves the goldest medal you've got. In the past I called her a magician, but that suggested there was something mystical about what she does. The truth is, she works really hard and is just so, so good at her job. She makes editing look easy, and I did not throw any softballs her way. We had to teach ourselves so much, learn everything and then condense that into a few hundred words to fill these tiny bios with as much information as possible. I am forever grateful for all her hard work and her patience with me.

David Caplan is like the cool breeze amid the chaos. His thoughtfulness and confidence that we were making something beautiful were a constant guiding light through the tempest of research. To have someone on my side with such expertise helped make all this so much easier.

Nicole Brown went so far above and beyond with the design of this book. She worked tirelessly to try out every colour sample I sent her, and she found ways to make all my ideas work. She painstakingly wrangled my messy files and was just an all-around amazing person to work with. Thank you to everyone at Little, Brown for welcoming me into your offices and for your support in making this thing happen.

My agent, Carrie Hannigan, has been with me from the beginning. She's the one person who has seen every angle of this process and knows everything it took to get this book completed. It's a really exciting and sometimes nerve-racking journey, and I wouldn't, for one second, want to be on it alone. She and the team at HSG are my rock. Thanks to Jesseca Salky for her guidance and support. Ellen Goff was my hero in my time of need – I threw so much at her: art questions, fact checking, costume advice and she delivered.

Thank you to all the people who helped me find names and track down odd bits of research, and provided personal and professional expertise along the way: Anna Barnes, Anna Prendella, Jen Graham, Erika Schwartz, Azadeh Navai, Arpita Kumar, Kevin Everson, Kwesi Johnson and Betzy Bromberg.

As always, I owe the biggest thank-yous to Ted, Chandra and Nicole Harrison, who are my biggest fans and strongest supporters, my sounding boards and strategists.

Lastly, to the girls and women in the world making things, experimenting and asking questions, I just want to say thank you for being brave enough to follow your passions and dream big.

Nicole Harrison

VASHTI HARRISON is an artist and film-maker with a passion for storytelling. She earned her BA in studio art and media studies from the University of Virginia and her MFA in film/video from California Institute of the Arts, where she snuck into animation and illustration classes to learn from Disney and DreamWorks legends. There she rekindled a love for drawing and painting. Now she uses her love of both film and illustration to craft beautiful stories for children.

@vashtiharrison ✳ vashtiharrison.com